The Tax-Free
Business Owner

How Business Owners Can Use the Tax Code
to Legally Pay Zero Taxes

Mark Miller, RBFC

READ THIS FIRST!

If you're the type that likes to cut to the chase. Find out firsthand whether you'll qualify to save 10's of thousands in taxes this year:

Go directly to the author, Mark Miller's personal calendar for a complimentary, no-obligation 20-minute tax strategy session.

https://calendly.com/hiltonwealth/taxsaving

DISCLAIMER:

This book is for informational purposes only and does not constitute a complete description of all services provided by Mark Miller or Hilton Tax & Wealth Advisors, LLC. No information contained herein constitutes complete tax, legal, investment or insurance advice. This book should not be considered a solicitation, offer, or recommendation for the purchase or sale of any products and services discussed herein. Information throughout this book, whether stock quotes, charts, articles, or any other statement or statements regarding capital markets or additional tax and financial information, is obtained from sources that we, and our suppliers believe reliable, but we do not warrant or guarantee the timeliness or accuracy of this information. Neither we nor our information providers are liable for any errors or inaccuracies, regardless of cause, or the lack of timeliness of, or for any delay or interruption in the transmission thereof to the user. With respect to information regarding financial matters, nothing in this book should be interpreted as a statement or implication that past results are an indication of future performance.

Dedication

"I can think of no other God-given responsibility than to lend a helping hand to those in need." -Conrad Hilton

I am grateful for the opportunity to lend a helping hand, inspired by Conrad Hilton and the Hilton family. This book is dedicated to hard-working business owners who bring immense value to the marketplace. Over the past quarter-century, I have learned so much from your passion and drive. I hope the knowledge I share in this book can repay even a fraction of what you gave me. I am grateful for my wife, Kelly, my soulmate and the VP of Operations at Hilton Tax & Wealth Advisors. Her trustworthiness and dedication are unmatched. My children, Ainsley and Brooks, inspire me with their talents and aspirations. Lastly, my faith and relationship with my Heavenly Father shape my life. I am forever grateful for His blessings upon my family.

Contents

Part 1 – Welcome

Part 2 – The Power of Advanced Tax Planning

Part 3 – The Path Forward

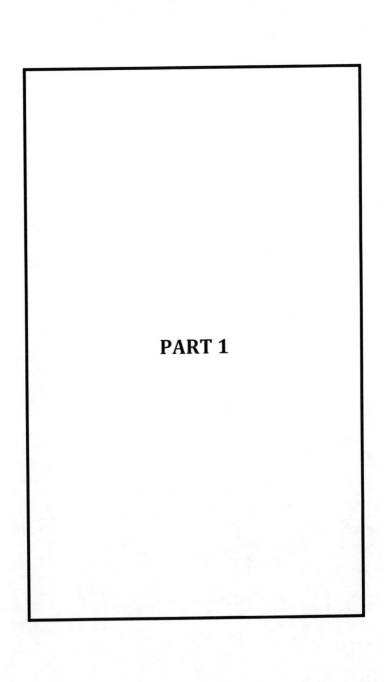

PART 1

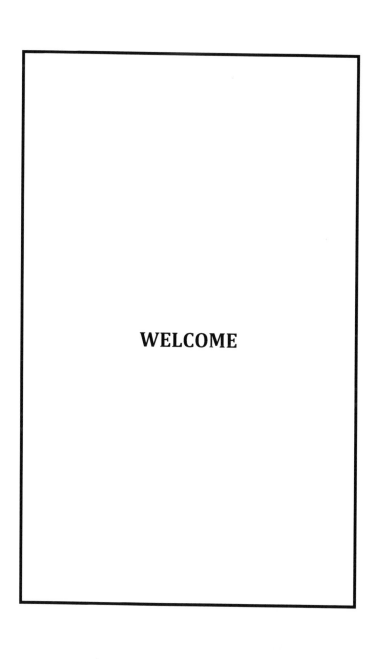

WELCOME

Who is This Book For?

In today's fast-paced world, we understand your time's value and want to ensure it is well invested. That's why it's essential to identify who will benefit most from reading this book. *The Tax-Free Business Owner* is designed specifically for business owners generating annual revenue of at least $500,000 and making combined federal and state tax contributions of $20,000 or more per year. While many of our clients surpass these thresholds, meeting these minimums is essential to leverage the strategies shared in this book fully.

Our journey begins by tackling your biggest expense—taxes. Understandably, the last thing you want to do with your hard-earned money is to part with it via tax payments. Uncle Sam, though a familiar figure, isn't always a welcomed guest in our financial affairs.

Many business owners are eager for PROACTIVE advice rather than reactive—guidance that illuminates the most recent tax savings and business expansion strategies. The Hiltons and I fervently believe in your right to lawfully and ethically minimize your tax liabilities to the least amount. A stance fortified for decades by numerous court decisions and IRS codes. This book serves as a guiding light for ambitious business owners who aspire to achieve the following:

• Craft a zero-tax plan that is not only ethical and legal but also built to withstand IRS scrutiny, ensuring peace of mind and financial stability.

• Potentially slash up to 99% of your capital gains tax when selling highly appreciated assets, such as your business, allowing you to unlock greater profits towards financial freedom.

• Connect with top-tier advisors, the very experts the ultra-rich employ to effectively eliminate your tax burdens and accelerate wealth creation.

• Lay a solid foundation for early retirement, supported by a steady stream of tax-free income that provides the security and comfort you deserve.

• Attain financial independence at a pace that surpasses your wildest dreams, granting you the power to dictate your desired lifestyle and pursue your passions.

These goals may appear ambitious, but rest assured; they are attainable—Hilton's track record attests to this. This concise yet powerful book unlocks the door to exclusive knowledge typically accessible only to billionaires and the ultra-affluent. Within its pages, you will gain profound insights into replicating the financial structures employed by esteemed families like our partners, the Hiltons. They allocate millions annually to their Family Office, granting them unparalleled access to top-tier financial resources.

I aim to serve as your trusted guide, helping you preserve and enhance your accumulated wealth. By implementing the strategies and principles outlined in this book, you can embrace a life where the fruits of your labor are fully enjoyed, your loved ones are well provided for, and your contributions to meaningful causes leave a lasting impact.

If these aspirations align with your own desires and ambitions, I wholeheartedly invite you to embark on this transformative journey with me. Together, we will delve deeper into the wealth-building strategies and insights that will shape your financial future. Prepare to unlock a world of possibilities and seize control of your financial destiny.

My Promise to You

This book exists for two reasons:

Reason #1: To inspire excitement in the powerful potential of proactive tax planning and specialized wealth planning. They both can help protect a significant part of your income and profits. This inspiration should motivate you to act on immediately

Reason #2 Being totally transparent...so that you may eventually hire me and my team to help you implement everything you read here.

Allow me to share a bit about myself to provide context and credibility to the insights we're offering.

As the president and CEO of Hilton Tax & Wealth Advisors, I proudly lead a distinguished team within the esteemed Hilton empire—a name you likely recognize from their renowned hotels and global presence. Our association with the Hilton family, who have amassed billions through strategic financial networks, grants us a unique advantage that can also extend to you.

Over the last several decades, I've had the privilege of contributing to numerous media outlets, such as The Wall Street Journal, Money and Kiplinger magazines, and even Fox News. I've earned the title of a best-selling author, and a few years back, I was honored as one of 50 recipients of the Presidential Businessman of the Year Award. This recognition was accompanied by a personal commendation from President George W. Bush for my contributions in aiding Americans to expand their businesses and wealth.

My intention isn't to boast but to emphasize the wealth of experience I bring, honed over a quarter-century. Having spent decades working closely with business owners and high-net-worth individuals like yourself on proactive tax and wealth building, I am confident in the insights I share. For instance, did you know that we employ over 110+ tax strategies, many of which most CPAs are either oblivious to or too complacent to leverage?

Prepare to learn the remarkable potential for tax savings that awaits you. On average, our clients experience annual tax savings of $30,192, and much more. These savings go far beyond what they imagined with their previous CPA alone. It's like uncovering a hidden treasure that was there all along, waiting to be discovered.

Imagine what you could do with this "found" money. You could reinvest it into your business, unlocking opportunities for growth and expansion. You could channel it towards personal endeavors, whether funding your dream vacation or supporting causes close to your heart. Finally, you could invest for a better future, securing a more comfortable lifestyle for you and your loved ones.

The possibilities are limitless, and we have seen the truly transformative impact. By taking advantage of these additional tax savings, you will seize the opportunity to unlock the full potential of your hard-earned income and accelerate your path to financial abundance.

Since you decided to read this book, I can infer something about you already:

1. **You're astute.** Your financial portfolio might not be as robust as you'd like, but it's not due to a lack of effort or attentiveness. You've heeded expert advice and implemented their strategies. You most likely consult with a CPA for tax preparation, engage a financial advisor, and keep abreast of market trends.

2. **You're diligent.** You've worked tirelessly and earned every cent you possess. Your financial success is a testament to your hard work and talents. I commend your relentless dedication to providing for your family and employees.

3. **You're pragmatic.** While a magical solution to financial prosperity might be appealing (if you happen to stumble upon such a genie, do share their contact!), you aren't relying on or actively seeking one. You appreciate truthful and solid financial data and have the acumen to make decisions based on that information.

So here lies my promise: Despite its brevity, this book is a powerhouse of invaluable insights that can echo through your financial journey for years. Every page turned is a step towards better tax management, greater wealth accumulation, and a more prosperous future for you and your business.

For more comprehensive information than what this book encapsulates, please visit our website at hiltonwealth.com or feel free to reach me personally at mmiller@hiltonwealth.com. You'll find a wealth of additional resources at your disposal.

Introduction

Cast your mind back to the exhilarating day when you stepped out from the crowd to launch your own business. That day, you courageously seized control of your destiny, setting a course for the uncharted waters of financial freedom. No longer content to be a cog in the wheel of someone else's dreams, you made the daring decision to turn your vision into reality.

Yet, as you continued on your entrepreneurial journey, you found yourself in the throes of bureaucratic red tape and regulatory challenges. Among them, one stood out like a sore thumb—taxes. The infamous certainty of taxes, immortalized in Benjamin Franklin's oft-quoted wisdom, *"In this world, nothing can be said to be certain, except death and taxes,"* suddenly became a daunting reality. Your fledgling business was not just dealing with vendors, clients, and employees but also facing the staggering responsibility of a mounting tax burden.

In our entrepreneurial roles, we are problem solvers, decision-makers, strategists, and much more. As our businesses blossom, it often seems our tax bills are on steroids, growing disproportionately, almost voraciously. Perhaps it feels as if this escalating tax demand has become an impediment to realizing your business aspirations and personal financial dreams.

The arrival of that first hefty tax bill can hit like a heavyweight champion, knocking the wind out of your sails. Desperate for some form of reprieve, you turn to trusted professionals - your accountant, attorney, or financial advisor. You hope for a lifeline, some sage advice. Instead, you're often met with a lukewarm reassurance about paying your fair share and a rather unsympathetic reminder of the bitter pill that success comes with a hefty tax bill. The common refrain is - that the more you earn, the more you owe Uncle Sam.

This scenario mirrors my experience from years ago. As my business flourished and my income rose, so did my tax liabilities exponentially. It felt like a raw deal, and I grappled with this disheartening reality. Despite my extensive financial education, why hadn't I been equipped with strategies to handle my tax liabilities effectively? Why hadn't I been privy to the inside scoop on how the ultra-wealthy use select tax minimization strategies, sometimes reducing their tax bill to an astonishing zero?

Fueled by an unwavering determination to safeguard a greater portion of my hard-earned profits, I fearlessly delved into the intricate realm of taxes. To my dismay, I uncovered a disconcerting truth: a startlingly small number of financial professionals, including those adorned with the esteemed CPA designation, possess the necessary expertise or inclination to assist entrepreneurs in navigating the complex web of taxes.

Undeterred by this revelation, I embarked on a self-guided expedition to master the art of proactive tax planning, and what an extraordinary journey it proved to be! With each step forward, I gained invaluable insights and honed my skills in uncovering innovative strategies to minimize my tax liability. The results were nothing short of remarkable.

In the first year alone, I witnessed my tax bill reduced by 50%. The impact was tangible and transformative, empowering me with newfound financial freedom and the ability to allocate my resources toward further growth and prosperity. But the journey did not end there.

Through persistent dedication and an unrelenting pursuit of knowledge, I continued to refine my tax planning strategies, ultimately reaching the coveted zero-tax bracket. Yes, you read that correctly—my tax obligations were eliminated entirely, freeing me from the burden that plagues so many business owners.

This journey of self-discovery and empowerment has taught me the immense value of proactive tax planning. It has proven that taking charge of our financial destiny and seeking unconventional solutions can lead to extraordinary results. Now, the Hiltons and I are committed to sharing these insights and strategies with fellow entrepreneurs like you so you, too, can experience the profound benefits of harnessing the power of tax optimization.

Here's a snapshot of the transformative journey that lies ahead:

Chapter 1, *"Isn't My CPA Already Doing ALL this for Me?"* will prompt a paradigm shift as we illuminate the truth about the role your CPA plays in your tax planning. You may discover gaps you never even knew existed.

Chapter 2, *"Debunked: Seven Myths About Tax Planning,"* will shatter commonly held fallacies about tax planning that could have been silently draining your wealth.

Chapter 3, *"The Secret to How the Ultra-Affluent Protect Their Wealth,"* opens the door to a world of elite financial strategies, providing you with a rare opportunity to learn from the wealthiest and put their methods into practice.

Chapter 4, *"What Matters Most to You About Wealth?"* we plunge into the heart of your dreams and aspirations. Unearthing your unique definition of wealth is key to shaping a financial strategy that aligns with your deepest values.

Chapter 5, "*Why the Hiltons and I are Uniquely Qualified to Help*," uncovers why our distinctive combination of knowledge, hands-on experience, and premier connections makes us the perfect allies in your quest for financial freedom.

This book is the key that unlocks the door to a transformative financial future. As you immerse yourself in its pages, we will navigate uncharted territories together, illuminating the path to tax optimization and more creative wealth creation.

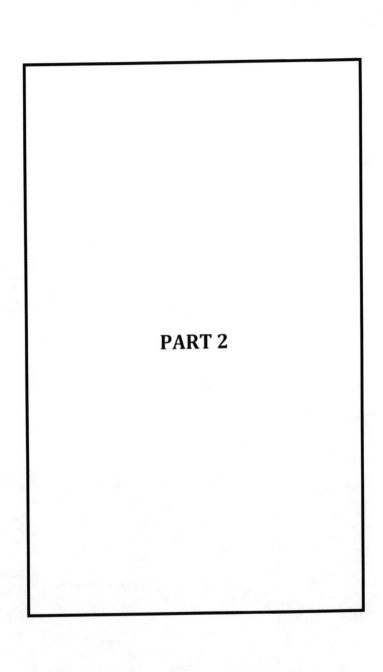

PART 2

THE POWER OF
ADVANCED TAX PLANNING

Chapter 1

Isn't My CPA Already Doing All This for Me?

"Insanity is doing the same thing over and over and expecting different results."
– Albert Einstein

I magine setting out on a road trip without a clear destination or roadmap. If that sounds frustrating, it's because it is. For many business owners, however, this metaphor mirrors their current tax situation, a journey without a strategic guide. It's a common misconception among today's successful business owners that their CPA is that guide, delivering innovative tax and financial ideas whenever needed. In reality, this assumption is rarely the case.

Traditional CPAs are stretched to their limits. Engulfed in a whirlwind of responsibilities, they produce an overwhelming volume of tax returns and financial statements annually. Often, they find themselves swamped with small clients whose revenue barely justifies the time invested. Their primary function isn't proactive tax planning but a rather mechanical process of recording past years' financial history for their clients. This is much like a more advanced iteration of TurboTax. They ensure numbers align, forms are completed correctly, and deadlines for tax return filings are met - essentially, compliance work.

Consider their workday. CPAs dive into pile after pile finalizing a batch of client tax returns. It's an unending cycle of monotony, mirroring the relentless cycle of Groundhog Day during tax season. Once they establish the prior year's tax history, there's little time for significant alterations. While some might recommend last-minute contributions to a 401(k) or IRA or change your business entity, they don't generally offer more innovative strategies. It's as if they are driving a car using only the rear-view mirror, focusing solely on what's behind rather than what lies ahead. Insanity.

Now, don't misunderstand me. The recording of financial history is undeniably crucial. Both you and the IRS need to know your exact income from the previous year. However, as you climb the ladder of success and income and taxes rise, your focus naturally has to shift. It's no longer just about knowing how much you owe; comprehending how to reduce this tax burden becomes increasingly essential. Regrettably, this insight is not typically provided by most accountants.

While it may seem like I'm casting CPAs in an unflattering light, it's important to clarify that my goal is not to criticize. We actively collaborate with CPAs in our firm. My aim here is to provide an insider's perspective to illuminate their true function. CPAs are incredibly intelligent individuals, but they operate within an industry bound by tradition and norms that hinder innovation. The business model that has served the accounting profession for over a century is showing its age, and despite your fondness for your CPA, their model isn't built to enrich you.

Consider the US Tax Code, one of the most intricate legal documents ever crafted, with an estimated count of over 150,000 pages, a number that continues to grow. This complex and ever-evolving legal maze presents unique opportunities for those adventurous enough to delve into proactive tax planning.

When seeking proactive ways to pay less tax, the standard CPA response is to increase your retirement plan contributions. They view this as a simple, effective method to defer your current tax liability. This may seem like a solution at the time, but it just postpones the problem.

I often ask my clients this simple yet crucial question: if you were a farmer, would you prefer to pay taxes on the seed or the crop? Almost always, they choose the seed.

The goal is not simply to defer taxes and delay the inevitable but to be proactive in managing your tax liabilities and maximizing your after-tax wealth on the front end. It requires a shift in mindset. Trusting in the power of proactive tax planning can help you cultivate a thriving financial landscape where the goal is to minimize your tax burden so your wealth can flourish.

So, when considering the farmer's dilemma of the seed or crop, remember the wise choice lies in optimizing your tax strategy from the beginning. By doing so, you can nurture financial growth while avoiding the pitfalls of burdensome taxes down the road.

Embracing Proactive Planning

As we conclude this exploration into the role of a traditional CPA, it's time for introspection - to locate your current position on the map of your financial journey. Are you content with using the rear-view mirror to guide your financial decisions, or do you feel compelled to shift gears and pioneer a more forward-looking approach? Now is the moment to challenge your existing tax planning strategy and open your mind to the potential of proactive planning.

As we embark on the next phase of our journey together, we'll debunk common myths, expose hidden truths about tax planning, and let these questions guide our way. Keep them close, for they will serve as the pillars of the proactive approach we will delve into in the coming chapters. Remain open-minded, curious, and ready for change as we venture towards a more empowered and prosperous financial future.

Client Case File

Matt K. - Unlocking Hidden Savings and Unleashing Business Potential

Overview: Matt K. is the visionary entrepreneur behind a pioneering IT outsourcing company based in Bangladesh. Since its establishment in 2006, Matt's company has delivered many IT-oriented services, including Web and Software Development, Quality Assurance testing, Digital Advertising Operations, Data Cleansing, Analysis, and Back Office Processing. By offering highly educated and hard-working professionals, Matt's firm provides clients with a competitive advantage, enabling them to save time and money on high-value IT services while redirecting their resources to more profitable tasks. As a result of their exceptional performance, Matt's company has garnered international recognition, being named one of the top 100 outsourcing companies in the world by the International Association of Outsourcing Professionals in 2014.

Challenges and Solutions

Despite his company's success, Matt felt that his previous tax and financial advisors lacked the creative thinking and innovative strategies he sought to optimize his business operations. Although he appreciated their efforts, he realized he was constantly brainstorming ideas while his advisors merely followed his lead. Determined to discover a team that could match his entrepreneurial mindset, Matt learned about Hilton Tax & Wealth Advisors through a trusted friend.

Impressed by the Hilton team's business-oriented approach, Matt decided to make the switch. He yearned for advisors who could not only provide tax and financial expertise but also challenge him with fresh ideas and uncover significant savings opportunities. Collaborating with Hilton, Matt discovered a world of untapped potential.

Results

Within just one year of working with Hilton Tax & Wealth Advisors, Matt experienced a transformational journey. The Hilton team delved deep into his business, identifying safe and innovative ways to maximize tax savings and improve his bottom line. Matt was thrilled with the outcomes, regretting only that he hadn't found Hilton earlier, as the potential savings could have amounted to millions. Nevertheless, he expressed gratitude for having Hilton on his team and acknowledged the profound impact they had on his business.

Today, Matt continues to work hand in hand with the Hilton team, benefiting from their strategic thinking, in-depth industry knowledge, and commitment to his success. With Hilton's guidance, Matt is unlocking hidden savings, gaining financial peace of mind, and confidently steering his business toward continued growth and prosperity.

Conclusion

Matt's journey with Hilton Tax & Wealth Advisors exemplifies the power of aligning with a team of advisors who not only understand the unique needs and aspirations of business owners but also possess the expertise and creativity to unleash their full potential. With Hilton by his side, Matt has discovered a wealth of opportunities he never thought possible, and he looks forward to an even brighter future propelled by innovative strategies and substantial tax savings.

Chapter 2

Debunked:
Seven Myths About Tax Planning

Theodore Roosevelt once quipped, *"Taxes are the price we pay for a civilized society."* But what if that "price tag" was negotiable and the new price completely above board? What if the Byzantine world of taxes concealed opportunities for savings, merely waiting for discovery? Now is the moment to overturn antiquated assumptions, and that's precisely why we're here.

Regrettably, many CPAs simply lean on IRS-provided literature for guidance on surrendering their money to the government. Others attend seminars and classes, hoping to decipher the convoluted tax rules and regulations. The pitfall of this approach is that most seminars simply drill down on what the IRS rules entail; they do not instruct CPAs on how to apply these rules to benefit their clients strategically.

Let's expose and dismantle seven enduring myths about tax planning, myths that your own CPA may be guilty of perpetuating.

Myth #1: "Implementing novel tax-saving strategies invites an audit!"

Let's address this prevailing myth about audits right from the start. The fear of audits shouldn't deter us from proactive tax planning. To think, *"If I adopt a different approach to lower my taxes, it will automatically trigger an audit,"* is an illusion created and sustained by some in the tax industry.

A change in strategy doesn't necessarily equate to an increased risk of audit. It's important to understand the difference between tax avoidance (legal) and tax evasion (illegal). As informed individuals, our goal is, naturally, legal tax avoidance.

Three primary ways facilitate this. Firstly, align with the IRS tax codes. For instance, availing yourself of a mortgage interest deduction as per the tax code doesn't escalate your audit risk, does it? Instead, it merely lowers your tax liability.

Secondly, consider case law. We employ strategies deemed acceptable by the IRS, as validated by case law. For example, if a corporation successfully defended its tax-saving actions in court, we can employ similar strategies backed by this legal precedent, strengthening our stance further.

Finally, we have Private Letter Rulings. These rulings, although issued privately, must be made public. So, when a significant player like Baron Hilton seeks IRS validation for a specific tax-saving strategy, the outcome informs everyone. This can provide us insights into the IRS's thought process and precedents.

At Hilton, we utilize a blend of these tools and supplements to benefit you. Here's an insider tip: Streamlining your taxes with a proactive tax plan will, of course, reduce your tax bill. But more surprisingly, in nine out of ten cases, this careful planning substantially diminishes the possibility of an audit.

Myth #2: "My CPA is already a tax wiz, wielding their expert powers to optimize my savings."

Does this sentiment resonate? Are you echoing declarations like, *"My CPA is a genius! Surely, there's nothing left for you to uncover, Mark."* Or perhaps, *"My brother-in-law, the city's leading CPA, couldn't overlook anything. He's already optimized my tax savings!"*

Let's flip this script, shall we?

Unsettlingly, the stark truth is that 95% of CPAs do not engage in any meaningful form of proactive tax planning. The belief that you've squeezed every penny of savings from your tax situation is often mistaken. Most of our clients, before consulting us, were inadvertently overpaying their taxes. Our diligent approach often reveals significant tax savings that highly-reputed CPAs might overlook. These discovered savings frequently surpass the cost of our services by a factor of ten, transforming our fees into a strategic investment rather than an expense.

Myth #3: "Home office deductions are a red flag...I'll for sure get audited."

Hold that thought! The real story is that home office deductions are not the audit magnets they've been portrayed as. The evolution of work, driven by the internet and accelerated by the global pandemic, means more of us are working from home than ever. Legal precedents exist where a doctor deducted not just his primary office but also his home office and the lake house office, winning against the IRS in court.

The tax code provides three clear pathways to home office deductions. How can they be considered 'red flags' when explicit directions for these deductions are embedded in the code itself?

Claiming your home office is not an invitation for trouble, provided it aligns with the tax code, is adequately documented, and is backed by case law. This issue hasn't been a concern for a considerable time. If your CPA hinders your utilization of these deductions, it might be time for a second opinion.

Myth #4: "It's not how much you make; it's how much you keep."

This phrase might sound like a nugget of wisdom, but it holds just some truth. Regarding taxes, a more accurate mantra would be: "It's not just how much you make or keep; it's HOW you earn it that matters."

This means that in the realm of tax planning, it's crucial to structure your earnings to maximize tax-free or tax-advantaged income proactively. Regrettably, you can't retroactively adjust how you earned your income to reap better tax benefits. The only way to manage this is through diligent and proactive (yes, that word again!) tax planning. It's a significant factor that can make a difference in your financial health.

Myth #5: "The 401(k) - The 'Superhero' of Retirement Savings."

You've likely heard it - from your CPA, from the media, from your friends: the 401(k) is the undisputed champion of retirement savings. Brace yourself because we'll pull the rug from under that claim. It's a myth, pure and simple, that the 401(k) is the unrivaled heavyweight contender in the retirement savings arena. In our playbook, the 401(k) is a bit-part player, a sidekick at best, brought in when it fits into a broader, more intelligent strategy.

Over the past several years, amid a pool of hundreds of affluent clients, we've barely had a handful of cases where we endorsed a 401(k) as a standalone solution. Yet, the common narrative pushed by CPAs and financial advisors endorses it as the one-size-fits-all, de facto company-sponsored plan.

But here's our different approach: we dance to the rhythm of the tax code, not the tune of products or the latest fad in retirement plans, including the glamorous 401(k). Our mission is your maximum savings, and the 401(k), often clunky and exorbitantly priced, hinders rather than aids this cause. It's not just an awkward fit for tax planning; it's essentially the square peg in the round hole of retirement savings.

This revelation may shock many, including industry insiders. But the truth, though unexpected, is the first step to smarter, more lucrative retirement planning.

Myth #6: "My regular medical expenses aren't deductible."

We get this one quite often. Much has changed in the medical world since Obamacare, as Obamacare's rules messed with medical deductions. But we have a popular strategy to save you a big chunk of your regular medical costs, over and above the cost of your medical insurance or deductibles. The tax code has some slick things (not just itemized deductions) to reduce your taxes on those medical expenses you thought weren't deductible. You're spending this money already, so wouldn't you want to make it ALL tax-deductible if you could?

Myth #7: "Tax planning isn't worth the time. My income is too high to design a plan to reduce my taxes."

I get this one on occasion because I work with a lot of highly successful business owners and high-net-worth individuals who might tell me: *"Look, Mark, I* *would rather just make a bunch more money, like $1,000,000 in new revenue, than worry about doing a bunch of tax strategies to save $200,000 in taxes."*

To which I'll respond, *"Well, a million dollars in revenue IS $200,000 in tax savings."*

IMPORTANT: If you get what I'm about to explain, it's ALL you need to read in this entire book to understand how powerful tax planning can be to your future.

Let's say you have a 20% profit margin. You make $1,000,000 in revenuc, so you'll net out $200,000. Are you ready for this? Deep, deep math (just kidding here). So, if I show you how to save $200,000 in taxes, it's the equivalent of earning $1,000,000 in revenue! Wouldn't you rather get the easy tax savings instead of working your butt off to generate that much more revenue? Remember what I wrote about earlier: "found" money.

Better yet, if you're an optimist like me, why not do both? Earn the extra $1,000,000 (On Hilton's business planning side, we'll help you grow your business in many other ways to make that happen).

But you can also save hundreds of thousands in taxes as icing on the cake. This money you can put right back in your pocket! Your profit margin will increase, and your bottom line will improve. All because of proper tax planning. This is just being smart.

Moving Beyond the Myths

We've just debunked a series of myths that have led many business owners and individuals astray, causing them to leave massive sums of money on the table - or worse, in the hands of the tax collector. By now, you should feel a sense of excitement, if not shock, at the sheer potential of strategic tax planning.

Reflect on this - how have these myths influenced your tax planning strategy up until now? How many opportunities have you missed to increase your bottom line by simply tweaking your tax approach? Now that you know that your regular medical expenses can be fully deductible and that your income level does not impede reducing your taxes, what will you do differently?

Consider the unexpected revelation that saving $200,000 in taxes equals earning a million in revenue. Are you ready to shift your focus from generating more revenue to strategic tax planning?

As we gradually peel away each layer of misconceptions, we reveal more of the tax code's true depth and complexity. And, as you have seen, within that complexity lie opportunities for significant savings. With this knowledge, are you ready to change your tax strategy?

As we move forward, prepare to uncover even more surprising truths about how the ultra-affluent protect their wealth. The next chapter reveals the secret mechanisms by which some of the world's wealthiest individuals legally pay virtually zero taxes. In contrast, hardworking individuals like yourself may pay up to 60% of their income in taxes.

It's time to pull back the curtain on the two-tiered taxation system and discover how you can tap into these strategies and protect your wealth.

Client Case File

Dr. Ron P. - Transforming Lives and Maximizlng Financial Success

Overview

Dr. Ron P. is not your typical orthodontist. With over four decades of experience, he has established himself as an expert in resolving complex orthodontic issues. However, Dr. Ron's dedication to continuous learning led him to make a remarkable discovery. He observed that many patients with jaw joint or TMJ problems also suffered from sleep disorders. Leveraging his expertise, Dr. Ron developed a groundbreaking treatment approach that combines orthodontics with oral appliances, achieving remarkable success rates in improving the quality of his patients' lives. Passionate about helping people sleep better, Dr. Ron aims to transform lives and eradicate unnecessary suffering.

Solutions

Recognizing the need for comprehensive tax mitigation and wealth planning, Dr. Ron turned to Hilton Tax & Wealth Advisors, drawn by the exclusive offerings of the Hilton Family Office. He understood that these were strategies utilized by the wealthiest individuals, which were typically out of reach for small business owners like himself. Excited by the opportunity, Dr. Ron eagerly engaged Hilton's services, knowing their expertise would result in substantial tax savings.

Through Hilton's tax planning services, Dr. Ron experienced tangible financial benefits, saving tens of thousands of dollars annually achieved with complete transparency and ethical practices. The newfound savings bolstered his practice's bottom line, providing him with peace of mind and allowing him to focus on what he loves most—improving the lives of his patients. Encouraged by the success of their initial collaboration, Dr. Ron and Hilton set their sights on a comprehensive succession plan, charting a path for an early exit from his medical practice.

Results

While Dr. Ron's journey with Hilton Tax & Wealth Advisors is still in progress, the early stages have already yielded impressive results. Through meticulous planning, Hilton has identified additional tax savings opportunities, further enhancing Dr. Ron's financial success. These efforts have culminated in annual tax savings exceeding $100,000, a testament to Hilton's expertise and commitment to their clients' prosperity.

In addition to tax optimization, Hilton recognized the untapped potential of Dr. Ron's practice and devised a strategy to leverage best-in-class online marketing experts. This approach is poised to double Dr. Ron's client base, propelling his practice into the modern era and ensuring long-term growth and success.

Conclusion

Dr. Ron's collaboration with Hilton Tax & Wealth Advisors exemplifies the power of strategic planning and expert guidance in maximizing financial success. By tapping into the exclusive offerings of the Hilton Family Office, Dr. Ron gained access to strategies typically reserved for the ultra-affluent. The substantial tax savings, combined with the implementation of advanced marketing techniques, have not only bolstered his financial bottom line but also positioned his practice for exponential growth.

As Dr. Ron continues his journey with Hilton, he looks forward to further uncovering the hidden possibilities within his practice and realizing his dream of an early exit, all while providing exceptional care to his patients. The transformative impact of Hilton's expertise has allowed Dr. Ron to fulfill his passion, change lives, and secure his financial future.

Chapter 3

The Secret to How
The Ultra-Affluent
Protect Their Wealth

"In America, there are two tax systems: one for the informed and one for the uninformed." - Learned Hand, Judge, United States Court of Appeals for the Second Circuit.

In 2007, Jeff Bezos, a multi-billionaire and the world's third richest person, paid not a single penny in federal income taxes. He achieved this feat again in 2011. In 2018, Tesla founder Elon Musk, the second-richest individual globally, also paid no federal income taxes. Michael Bloomberg, billionaire investor Carl Icahn, and George Soros all managed to do the same in recent years.

Surprisingly, Warren Buffett, the centibillionaire with a grandfatherly image, avoided the most tax among the 25 wealthiest individuals. This is quite unexpected, given his public stance as an advocate of higher taxes for the wealthy.

According to Forbes, Buffett's fortune increased by $24.3 billion between 2014 and 2018. Over those years, he reported paying only $23.7 million in taxes, resulting in a true tax rate of 0.1% or less than ten cents for every $100 he added to his wealth.

These examples shatter the myth of the American tax system that everyone pays their fair share and the wealthiest pay the most. IRS records reveal that the wealthiest individuals can legally pay income taxes that are only a fraction of the millions or billions their fortunes grow yearly. How you might ask, is it possible, let alone legal, for such gross disparities to exist within the tax system of the United States of America?

Proactive Versus Advanced Tax Planning: A Tale of Two Towns

Let's take a trip into two unique towns, Proactiveville and Advancedville, to better understand the difference between proactive and advanced tax planning.

Imagine Proactiveville as a vibrant town where the residents, just like its name suggests, are always one step ahead. They keep an eagle's eye on their yearly calendar, marking potential tax implications on every financial move they make. Like a diligent gardener who prunes their plants throughout the year, these residents frequently review and adjust their financial actions in response to the changing seasons of tax laws. They seek all legal avenues to reduce their tax liability, like a smart shopper who never misses a chance to use a discount coupon. This is the essence of proactive tax planning.

Now, let's journey to Advancedville. This town might look similar to Proactiveville at first glance. However, it houses larger estates and businesses with complicated financial landscapes. Here, the townsfolk play a different kind of game. It's not just about yearly pruning or using every coupon - it's more like chess, plotting multiple moves well ahead. They deploy sophisticated strategies, such as shifting income to different years, managing capital gains, planning their estates, or setting up charitable trusts. They work with expert tax advisors, akin to skilled architects who can find hidden pathways in a labyrinth of laws and regulations. This is the realm of advanced tax planning.

While Proactiveville and Advancedville share a common goal of tax reduction, they represent different levels of engagement and expertise in handling tax matters. Some people might feel at home in either town, both proactive and advanced tax planning can coexist in your financial strategy. But remember, while Proactiveville is a town anyone can live in with some effort, Advancedville is a place you need a team of qualified experts to help you navigate effectively.

Unlocking Hidden Treasures: The Importance of True Due Diligence in Advanced Tax Planning

Let's take a trip back to your childhood, but this time, we're not just heading to a familiar school classroom. Imagine that instead, our playground is an expansive corn maze. You and your classmates are excited to explore this mysterious labyrinth. It's an adventure full of twists, turns, and countless dead-ends. This is the complex landscape of advanced tax planning.

In this maze, there's a rumored hidden treasure - rare, valuable gems that could unlock untold wealth. But they're not scattered along the path or sitting in open sight; they're concealed within the maze's walls, accessible only to those with a detailed map and the will to uncover them.

This is where 'Due Diligence' comes into play. In the context of tax planning, it means carefully examining every twist and turn, inspecting each wall of the corn maze for potential hidden gems, and charting a safe path to acquire them.

But remember, not everyone in the maze has the same tools, knowledge, or even the will to uncover these hidden gems. You see your classmates spread out through the maze. Some are playing tag, others are tracing the outer edges, and a few are aimlessly wandering, oblivious to the potential treasures around them.

However, a few students are equipped with detailed maps and mining tools, meticulously examining every inch of the maze, unearthing these rare gems. These are the tax professionals with a true understanding of due diligence. They're like the industrious miners sifting through piles of rubble to discover a hidden vein of gold.

As we step into the modern-day, the corn maze transforms into the tax planning landscape of today, and those classmates grow into the tax advisors, CPAs, and lawyers you might see. And just like in the corn maze, not all professionals are equipped to practice true due diligence.

Many financial institutions, such as Goldman Sachs or Deloitte, operate like maze-runners with blinders, focused only on the paths they've been told to follow. They adhere to their internal protocols and products, shying away from innovative strategies that might lie outside their familiar route.

They're sticking to a well-trodden path in the corn maze, ignoring potential treasure hiding just off the beaten path. And why wouldn't they? Exploring the entire maze requires resources, knowledge, and an element of risk that many are unwilling or unable to shoulder.

But the real challenge is that the true pathfinders of the tax world, specialized tax attorneys with intimate knowledge of the maze, are bound by law to work in the shadows. They're like the legendary map-makers of old, unable to advertise their trade or share their knowledge with the general public.

This reality underscores the importance of having an expert tax advisor who can navigate the tax maze, has the tools to unearth the hidden gems, and understands the laws that govern this complex landscape. In the labyrinth of advanced tax planning, true due diligence is the map to the hidden treasures, and few are equipped to use it effectively.

Specialist Tax Attorneys and the Limitations on Sharing Expertise

To add another layer of complexity to the pursuit of effective tax solutions, specialist tax attorneys, the hidden champions of tax optimization for billionaires, are bound by legal restrictions that prevent them from marketing their expertise to the general public.

This legal barrier makes it incredibly challenging for the average CPA or tax advisor to discover new, potentially advantageous strategies for their clients. It's like trying to unearth hidden gems without a map or knowing they exist.

Family Offices vs. Traditional Retail Wealth Management Firms

So, how do traditional CPAs or tax advisors discover these optimal solutions for their clients?

The answer lies in plain sight, in an exclusive establishment called the Family Office.

Family Offices might as well be phantom entities for most of the public, given their elusive nature. More concerning is that a significant proportion of financial professionals are oblivious to the existence and the purpose of Family Offices. Yet, these entities are the chosen financial stewards for renowned individuals such as Michael Jordan, Bill Gates, and Oprah Winfrey.

Imagine a Family Office as a bespoke financial concierge service for the ultra-wealthy. They offer an all-encompassing financial management solution, serving as personal CFOs. Their services span investment strategies, philanthropic guidance, budgeting, insurance, tax planning, and generational wealth management. Think of them as the all-in-one, 360-degree financial advisors for the ultra-affluent.

A Family Office is akin to having a customized roadmap, a well-stocked toolbox, and a seasoned guide navigating the complex tax maze. Sounds appealing, right?

Contrast this with traditional retail wealth management firms, like Charles Schwab, Merrill Lynch, or Fidelity Investments, which often lack of unique specialization in areas such as tax planning, philanthropy, and generational wealth management. It's like comparing a mom-and-pop store to a wholesale marketplace. We'd all prefer to access wholesale prices, given the resources. Likewise, in the financial world, Family Offices represent the wholesale option for those with the means.

Family Offices assemble a team of diverse experts under one roof, facilitating collaborative planning to preserve and grow the client's wealth. They ensure every twist and turn of the tax maze is meticulously explored to find the best possible route.

The adage "the rich get richer" rings true here. Access to a Family Office equips the affluent with industry-leading experts, fund managers, and resources - a luxury often beyond the reach of an average retail consumer. It's another secret passage in the tax maze that, until now, has been hidden from sight.

Two Tax Systems: The Choice between Informed Navigation or Uninformed Compliance

In conclusion, the veil shrouding the methods used by the ultra-affluent to safeguard their wealth has been lifted, revealing the mastery of navigation through the tax maze - a skill that distinguishes the informed from the uninformed.

For decades, the tax codes of America have been expertly wielded as tools by the ultra-wealthy, exemplified by business magnates such as Jeff Bezos, Elon Musk, and Warren Buffett, who have managed to minimize their tax liabilities significantly. How do they achieve this? It lies not in breaking the rules but in understanding and applying them with unrivaled finesse and forward-thinking strategy.

By unraveling these secrets, Hilton acknowledging that the tax maze is not a monolith; it is not a one-size-fits-all system where everyone pays their 'fair share.' Instead, it is a complex labyrinth with secret passages and hidden treasures that the ultra-affluent, guided by their skilled advisors, successfully navigate.

This is not a criticism of the rich but a lesson to be learned. Wealth protection is not a privilege reserved solely for the ultra-affluent. It is an art that can be mastered with the right guidance and understanding. The key is to arm oneself with knowledge, surround oneself with the right experts, and not be afraid to venture into the labyrinth. For it is only by understanding the game's rules that one can begin to play it effectively.

In the end, it is true: there are two tax systems, one for the informed and one for the uninformed. The question now is, which one will you choose to navigate?

Client Case File

"From Tax Efficiency to Financial Freedom: Dr. Nathan T.'s $100,000+ Annual Savings and Guaranteed Early Retirement"

Overview

Dr. Nathan T. is a highly accomplished medical professional, graduating Cum Laude and specializing in minimally invasive gynecologic surgery, obstetrics, and bioidentical hormone replacement. With a deep commitment to providing comprehensive gynecologic care throughout all stages of a woman's life, Dr. Nathan and his dedicated staff strive to ensure every patient's experience is comfortable and well-informed.

Solutions

Dr. Nathan initially had reservations about submitting his tax returns for review, given the utmost importance of confidentiality in the medical field. However, recognizing the critical need for creative tax and wealth planning, particularly due to the growth of their two medical practices, he sought the expertise of Hilton Tax & Wealth Advisors. Dissatisfied with the minimal tax planning offered by their previous advisors, Dr. Nathan and his wife were eager to explore Hilton's best-in-class solutions across the board.

Hilton's team implemented four key tax-saving strategies, resulting in annual savings of $100,000+. Additionally, they provided comprehensive guidance on business and personal wealth plans, restructuring debt, and developing proper exit and estate planning. Access to the wealth-building benefits of the Hilton Family Office further fortified their financial position. In total, Hilton's strategies are projected to put approximately $1-$3 million back into their pockets for retirement, all achieved at a fraction of the cost to benefits received. Found money.

Results

By partnering with Hilton Tax & Wealth Advisors, Dr. Nathan and his wife have experienced significant financial gains and are now equipped with a solid plan for their early retirement. The implementation of Hilton's wealth-building strategies has not only made their businesses tax-efficient but also paved the way for long-term growth and financial security.

With confidence and assurance, Dr. Nathan emphasizes the value Hilton has brought to their financial journey, stating, "Hilton Tax & Wealth Advisors has helped us implement and understand a wealth-building strategy that is guaranteed to grow our business." The expertise and guidance provided by Hilton have enabled them to maximize their wealth potential, ensuring a prosperous future.

Conclusion

Dr. Nathan's collaboration with Hilton Tax & Wealth Advisors exemplifies the transformative power of strategic tax and financial planning. By leveraging Hilton's expertise, Dr. Nathan and his wife have achieved substantial tax savings, optimized their business and personal wealth plans, and gained access to exclusive benefits through the Hilton Family Office. The profound impact of Hilton's tailored strategies will allow them to accumulate significant wealth, secure an early retirement, and fulfill their long-term financial goals.

The success story of Dr. Nathan stands as a testament to the exceptional value Hilton Tax & Wealth Advisors provides to medical professionals seeking comprehensive tax and wealth planning solutions. With Hilton by their side, Dr. Nathan and his wife have laid a solid foundation for their financial success, enabling them to focus on what they do best—providing exceptional care to their patients and embracing a bright and prosperous future.

Chapter 4

What Matters Most to You About Wealth?

"One should always play fairly when one has the winning cards." - Oscar Wilde

D o you remember your first tic-tac-toe game? I bet you lost. And do you know why? The one who taught you the game - they knew the tricks, they understood the strategy, and they had an unfair advantage. And here's the kicker: the same is true regarding wealth management.

See, the world's wealthiest have a secret playbook. It's not about earning more; it's about keeping more, managing risk, making intelligent investments, and planning for the future. Traditional wealth advisors? They're good, but they're playing checkers while the rich are mastering chess.

Your CPA is likely an excellent, friendly accountant and someone you should trust when filing your yearly tax returns and paying your quarterly estimates. But he or she doesn't have access to 500+ elite CPAs, attorneys, and other specialists whose sole focus is vetting advanced tax mitigation strategies for business owners like you.

Beyond Profits and Taxes: Unleashing the Power of Wealth and Legacy

Indeed, the journey to success as a business owner extends far beyond a well-optimized tax strategy. It intertwines deeply with how you envision and manage your life and the legacy you want to leave behind. It's not merely about surviving but genuinely thriving without the constant apprehension of your financial resources drying up. It's about living with the freedom to make choices that align with your desires and values, unencumbered by financial uncertainty and fear.

However, to achieve this state of financial liberation and security, one needs to weave a robust financial plan that goes beyond the immediate and looks ahead into the long term. A well-structured financial plan, much like a navigational chart, helps you map your course through life's financial journey, ensuring that you have enough to sustain your desired lifestyle, fulfill your life's ambitions, and secure your future.

Think of it as a three-dimensional puzzle. One dimension represents your income and wealth creation through your business endeavors. The second dimension is wealth preservation and growth, where tax optimization, investment strategies, and wealth management come into play. The third dimension, often overlooked, is wealth succession or legacy building. This dimension represents your aspirations to make a meaningful and lasting impact on the world that survives long after you're gone.

Building a legacy isn't just about accumulating and passing on wealth. It's about imprinting your values, teachings, and experiences onto future generations, shaping their lives and potentially the lives of many others. This could manifest in various forms - maybe you wish to establish a scholarship fund to support talented but economically disadvantaged students, or perhaps you dream of funding a medical research center. Your legacy could also be your successful business, handed down to your successors, continuing to grow and evolve with the changing times.

In essence, building a legacy is about the conscious decisions you make to ensure that your life's work and ethos continue to impact and influence the world positively long after your time. It's about creating something timeless and significant that echoes your life's purpose, beliefs, and passion.

However, shaping such a legacy requires thoughtful planning, starting with understanding the purpose of your wealth. It entails identifying your long-term goals and values and aligning your financial strategy accordingly. For this, you need a team of experts, including estate planners, tax advisors, and legal consultants, to help you navigate the complex landscapes of wealth succession, tax laws, and legal structures.

An adept team can help devise strategies to minimize estate taxes, avoid probate, and establish trusts or foundations as per your legacy aspirations. They can help align your business plans with your succession plans, ensuring a smooth transition that protects the business's value and continuity. A trusted advisor can also guide you to leverage philanthropy for tax benefits while contributing meaningfully to causes you are passionate about.

To summarize, being a successful business owner goes far beyond maximizing profits and minimizing taxes. It's about creating a financially secure life that allows you to live out your dreams without fear or uncertainty. It's about nurturing your wealth, so it not only serves you and your lifestyle but also paves the way for a significant and enduring legacy. After all, success is not just about the wealth you accumulate but also the impact you create and the legacy you leave behind.

The Wealth Priorities Quiz: Unveiling Your Path to Business Success, Family Security, and Lasting Legacy

As business owners, our financial journeys are as unique as the enterprises we build, intertwining the needs and priorities of our businesses, families and the legacy we strive to leave behind. It's time to unlock the secrets that drive your financial decisions and embark on a transformative journey of self-discovery. Allow "The Wealth Priorities Quiz" to guide you through a series of thought-provoking questions, revealing the path to effective wealth management tailored to your entrepreneurial aspirations.

Take a moment to assign a score of 1 (least Important) to 5 (most Important) based on your immediate response to each question. With each thoughtful answer, you'll gain valuable insights into your financial landscape, equipping yourself with the knowledge to shape a robust plan that aligns perfectly with your business goals, family security, and legacy-building vision.

Liquidity: Safeguarding Your Business and Family

How crucial is immediate access to funds for unforeseen expenses, ensuring the safety and security of your business and family? Consider the significance of maintaining a financial safety net, empowering you to seize opportunities and navigate unexpected challenges confidently.

Score: ___

Growth: Charting Your Business's Financial Future

How important is witnessing substantial growth in your business's wealth? Reflect on your comfort level with market risks and the extent to which you are willing to invest strategically, laying the foundation for long-term prosperity and sustainable success.

Score: ____

Income or Cash Flow: Sustaining Your Business and Lifestyle

How vital is the stability of your business's income or cash flow to support your desired lifestyle and fuel your entrepreneurial pursuits? Assess the significance of consistent cash flow in empowering your present and future business and personal needs.

Score: ____

Preservation: Safeguarding Your Business and Personal Wealth

How significant is preserving your business and personal wealth to you? Consider the value you place on minimizing losses and protecting your hard-earned assets, even if it might mean forgoing potentially higher returns, as you navigate the dynamic financial landscape.

Score: ___

Debt: Liberating Your Business Finances

How crucial is it for you to reduce or eliminate business and personal debts, freeing your enterprise financially? Assess the impact of existing financial obligations on your business's growth and explore strategic pathways toward debt liberation.

Score: ___

Heirs & Beneficiaries: Forging Your Family Legacy

How important is it for you to craft a lasting legacy and secure the financial well-being of your heirs and beneficiaries? Envision the role you want your wealth to play in the lives of your loved ones, leaving a positive and impactful footprint for future generations to cherish.

Score: ___

Total Score: ___

Upon totaling your scores, you'll gain profound insights into your financial focus and priorities:

- A score of 6-12 suggests a stronger emphasis on immediate needs and short-term goals. Consider aligning your strategies to incorporate long-term planning and growth for enhanced success, both personally and professionally.

- A score of 13-18 indicates a balance between short-term and long-term goals. Explore opportunities further to align your strategies with your overarching wealth objectives, fostering sustainable growth and stability.

- A score of 19-24 reflects a comprehensive grasp of your financial priorities, demonstrating an alignment with long-term goals and a proactive approach to wealth management. Fine-tune your strategies for even better outcomes, ensuring continued success and prosperity.

- A score of 25-30 signifies a holistic view of your financial priorities, showcasing a strong emphasis on long-term objectives and the creation of a lasting legacy. Celebrate your commitment to financial excellence and explore opportunities to maximize the impact of your wealth for generations to come.

From Insight to Application: Crafting Your Path to Financial Mastery

Unlocking the full potential of your wealth doesn't just come from understanding your priorities but also from developing a strategic, comprehensive, and personalized plan to put your insights into action. Navigating the complexities of financial management requires not just a roadmap but a seasoned guide who can help you traverse the unique contours of your wealth landscape. Seeking unique expert advice is the key to unlocking a world of possibilities, aiding you to create a bespoke wealth management plan that aligns perfectly with your aspirations, risk tolerance, and financial goals.

In the world of finances, self-awareness is indeed the starting point. It sets the tone for how we perceive and interact with our financial world. Yet, understanding alone is insufficient; it must be matched with strategic application. The journey from insight to application demands thorough planning, astute decision-making, and constant monitoring. Each decision you make and each risk you take, brings you closer to your financial objectives, be it building a safety net, growing your wealth, or leaving a legacy.

Finally, the ultimate destination of this journey is financial freedom. It's about reaching a state where your wealth serves your lifestyle, not the other way around. It's about creating a legacy that resonates with your values and aspirations. It's about experiencing the joy of financial peace of mind, knowing you're well-prepared for the future, and your wealth is optimized to withstand market upheavals and life's uncertainties.

So, are you ready to take your financial journey to the next level? In the upcoming chapter, we delve into the reasons why the Hiltons and I are uniquely qualified to help you navigate this complex yet rewarding journey of advanced tax planning and synergistic wealth building. Just as Barbara Bush wisely said, *"Believe in something larger than yourself...get involved in the big ideas of your time."* The next chapter does just that. You don't want to miss it.

Chapter 5

Why The Hiltons and I
Are Uniquely Qualified to Help

"The future depends on what you do today." - Mahatma Gandhi

I n the spirit of big ideas, let me start with a story, a story about Barron Hilton, son of the famed hotelier Conrad Hilton. Barron, like his father, was a businessman of great vision. Not only did he elevate the Hilton Hotels Corporation into a multibillion-dollar enterprise, but he was also an early investor in a then-unknown credit card company—now known as Visa. But his visionary thinking didn't stop there.

Barron had a clear wealth management strategy in place. He took a step that was nothing short of remarkable. He left 97% of his net worth to the Conrad N. Hilton Foundation, a philanthropic organization his father had established. At Hilton Tax and Wealth Advisors, we are proud to give a portion of our profits to the Hilton Foundation. Barron's decision ensured that his wealth would serve a bigger purpose long after he was gone while also employing a strategic estate planning technique to minimize tax liabilities. This story beautifully captures the essence of this book: a blend of business growth, strategic investment, and intelligent planning for the future.

Much like Barron, you might have many advisors working in your domain. But what you need, as Barron needed, is a seamless integration of all these elements—tax savings, business growth, and wealth accumulation. We call this Synergistic Wealth Building, and it forms the core philosophy at Hilton Tax & Wealth Advisors.

Now, this book might be compact, but it is filled with big ideas that could save you substantial amounts in taxes year after year. Advanced tax planning is not just about reacting to tax liabilities—

it's about proactive, strategic thinking. As December 31 of this year fast approaches, the options available to control your tax situation begin to fade. It's about ensuring Uncle Sam doesn't overstay his welcome in your finances.

Your financial strategy, like Barron's, should be geared towards your dreams rather than the government's objectives. It's not about whether you like or dislike the federal government—it's about making your hard-earned money work for you.

And this is where we come in. At Hilton Tax & Wealth Advisors, we believe in working with those who share our values and resonate with our methodologies. Are you one of them? To help you decide, I'd like to invite you to learn more about who we are. Let's embark on this journey to financial empow1erment together.

How Main Street Business Owners Win the Tax and Money Game with the Hilton Family Office

Bid farewell to the limitations of your local CPA, tax attorney, or financial advisor. With the Hilton Family Office (HFO), you'll gain access to a league of the world's finest minds, working tirelessly around the clock to deliver advanced tax planning and wealth-building strategies. We've revolutionized this landscape, bringing the might of a world class Family Office directly to Main Street. You'll be astounded by this financial paradigm shift!

The Hilton Family Office is more than just an entity—it's a thriving community of over 500 esteemed tax professionals, tax attorneys, and Family Office leaders. Collaborating synergistically, we unite to provide clients with best-in-class, peer-reviewed solutions.

Let's explore some of the extraordinary benefits you'll enjoy with the HFO:

1. Time Savings and Expert Access:

- Effortlessly access a global network of top-tier resources and specialists who cater to multi-billion-dollar Family Offices.
- Obtain unparalleled answers and guidance with just a simple touch, saving you precious time.

2. **Seamless Collaboration and Efficiency:**

- Experience the seamless harmony of your trusted advisors working as a united TEAM on a single platform.
- Maximize efficiency as they collaborate and craft the most powerful solutions to your dynamic challenges.

3. **Unlock a Wealth of Strategies:**

- Open the doors to a treasure trove of robust tax and cost-saving strategies.
- Leverage over 110 dynamic tactics, which can be combined in various powerful ways to suit your unique circumstances.

4. **Stress Relief and Peace of Mind:**

- Bid farewell to financial stress as the world's most brilliant and forward-thinking professionals diligently solve your challenges efficiently.

- Revel in the tranquility of knowing that your financial matters are in the hands of the very best.

5. **Safeguard Your Financial Future:**

- Mitigate financial risks and secure your future through financial risk reduction techniques.
- Explore alternative investments via our Exclusive Private Family Office Network.
- Discover comprehensive Income & Tax Mitigation solutions.
- Implement business cost reduction techniques to optimize your financial performance.
- Plan for seamless wealth transfer to protect your assets and leave a lasting legacy.
- Navigate Liquidity Event Planning with ease, ensuring smooth transitions.
- Enjoy personalized concierge services tailored to your desires.

With the HFO, you gain access to these incredible advantages that will not only simplify your financial journey but also empower you to achieve your goals with confidence. Say goodbye to complexity and embrace a future where your financial success is supported by the world's best resources and strategies.

Final Thoughts

As we bring this chapter to a close, I want to commend you for reading this far, taking the first bold steps toward financial empowerment. You have gained valuable insights into the transformative power of strategic tax planning and wealth-building strategies, and you are now equipped with the knowledge to navigate the complex world of finance with confidence.

But knowledge alone is not enough—it is action that truly counts. The words you have read and the ideas you have absorbed are just stepping stones on the path to financial success. It is what you implement that will shape your future and unlock the full potential of your financial endeavors.

As you turn the page to the next chapter, you are standing at the precipice of opportunity. The next steps you take will determine the trajectory of your financial journey. It should be a moment of anticipation, filled with the promise of transformation and the possibility of realizing greater dreams.

In the upcoming chapter, we will explore the concrete actions you can take to solidify your financial foundation and propel yourself toward greater prosperity. The path may not always be easy, but with the proper guidance and a commitment to implementation, you can pave the way to a more fulfilling financial future.

So, take a deep breath, steel yourself for the journey ahead, and let's embark together on the next steps toward financial liberation and lasting wealth.

Client Case File

Kevin H.'s Journey from Hailstorm Havoc to Tax Planning Triumph

In the heart of urban architecture where steel giants kiss the clouds, Kevin - a pioneer in the commercial real estate sector - was navigating a storm of a different kind. His innovative business harnesses sophisticated weather technology to help commercial building owners understand and react promptly to devastating hailstorm damage. This savvy approach saved his clients over $35 million in two short years.

As his business blossomed, Kevin discovered that his tax situation was becoming increasingly complex. He had enlisted the services of a highly recommended CPA, who assured Kevin they were doing everything possible to save on his taxes. Yet Kevin found himself grappling with a lingering sense of doubt. Just as he had done with his hailstorm detection business, Kevin instinctively knew there had to be a better, more proactive solution. This entrepreneurial intuition led him to Hilton Tax & Wealth Advisors.

Choosing Hilton was a strategic move, a testament to Kevin's propensity for challenging the status quo and his unfettered pursuit of efficiency. Hilton's comprehensive approach to fiscal optimization and its reputation for successful client relationships resonated with Kevin's own business ethos.

Upon engaging Hilton's services, Kevin embarked on an empowering journey of tax planning. Just a taste of a few strategies Hilton helped with — we used medical expense and accountable plans, leveraged corporate fringe benefits, and maximized multiple deep deductions. Then skillfully used a C-Corporation to retain earnings at lower rates. By doing so, he unlocked significant savings.

Despite these efforts, Kevin faced challenges. His previous CPA warned him of potential audits triggered by these proactive approaches. Yet, Hilton's methodical plan included not only cutting his audit risk but also adding audit insurance to his plan - all the while completing all his personal and business tax returns for half of what his previous CPA charged.

The outcomes were transformational. Kevin managed to keep a substantial portion of his profits within his rapidly expanding business. Kevin's reaction to these results was one of empowerment and enthusiasm. As he looked to the future of his burgeoning business, he acknowledged the pivotal role that Hilton played in his tax planning journey. *"My business is growing very quickly,"* says Kevin, *"and I plan on picking the brain of Mark Miller's team throughout the years. Thanks, Hilton."*

Kevin's story underscores how forward-thinking tax planning can turbocharge business expansion. Like Kevin's game-changing approach to an overlooked industry problem, we at Hilton are set on reshaping tax planning for entrepreneurs nationwide. Our mission is to help them keep more of their earnings, laying the groundwork for them to construct their financial dynasties and lasting legacies.

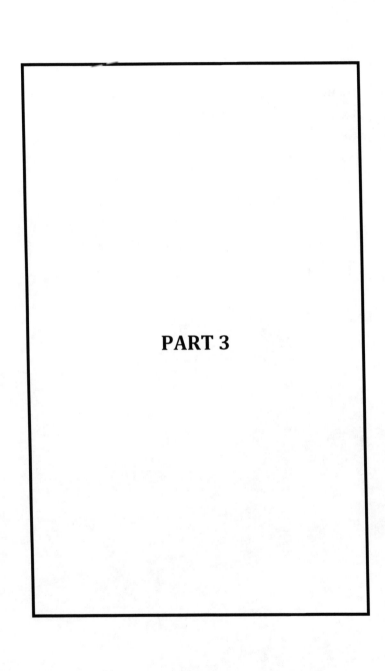

PART 3

THE PATH FORWARD

Chapter 6

The Next Step
Unlocking Your Financial Future

"It's not what you know; it's not even who you know; it's what you implement that counts." - Brian P. Moran

Congratulations! You have journeyed through the pages of this book, gaining valuable insights into advanced tax planning and wealth-building strategies. You are now one step closer to a life filled with happiness, adventure, and opportunity.

Take a moment to envision the future—imagine the peace of mind that comes from knowing your financial path is secure. Your family and legacy are protected, and true experts guide you. It's a gratifying feeling, and it makes the entire process of advanced tax and wealth planning worthwhile. As I mentioned at the outset, this book has two primary purposes:

1. To inform and motivate business owners like you.
2. To extend an invitation to explore the possibility of working together to create more profit, income, and wealth for you.

If you resonate with the ideas presented, you may be considering the option of working directly with Hilton. Perhaps you want to create or refine your tax and financial plan, ensuring it aligns with your long-term goals. Whether or not it makes sense for us to collaborate depends on your unique circumstances and aspirations. Allow me to pose three essential questions for your consideration:

1. Do you believe that taxes will continue to rise in the future?
2. Are you serious and committed to using the tax code to your advantage, legally, morally, and ethically, to create more income and

wealth for yourself and your family for years to come?

3. Do you value the guidance of genuine experts who will bring out your best and help you avoid costly mistakes?

If your answer to all three questions is a resounding "yes," then two pathways lie before you:

1. You can close this book, setting aside the information you have learned. However, if you have reached this point, I have a feeling this is not the option you desire.

2. You can take the proactive step of scheduling a complimentary 20-minute introductory phone call with me personally. This call will initiate the conversation, allowing us to determine whether you are a good candidate for our tax and wealth planning services.

If you are truly serious about securing your financial future, there is nothing to lose by choosing the second pathway. There is no cost or obligation, and scheduling the call is incredibly easy. Simply visit my calendar at calendly.com/hiltonwealth/taxsaving to select a day and time that suits you best.

Your goals are unique to you, so a conversation between us is crucial if you are committed to learning more about implementing the ideas shared in this book. The initial call is about helping you determine if working together is the right fit for you. It's about YOU and your aspirations.

I want to emphasize that this is NOT a sales call. It is a two-way interview, ensuring we agree on the best path forward. I will ask you questions, and you can ask me as many questions as you like. Together, we will decide the next steps.

Typically, this call lasts 20 minutes, but we will stay on the line until we determine whether it's a good fit. There is absolutely no obligation. Additionally, if you have any questions, email me directly at mmiller@hiltonwealth.com, call our office at (800) 691-6155 to set an appointment, or go to hiltonwealth.com to learn more.

Your financial empowerment is within reach; together, we can make it a reality. Take the next step. Your future awaits!

Resources & Social Media

In addition to the ideas and strategies I have already shared with you throughout this book, here are more resources:

Our Website:

https://www.hiltonwealth.com/

LinkedIn:

https://www.linkedin.com/in/markmiller-hiltonfo/

Additional Book Resources:

https://www.thetaxfreebusinessownerbook.com/resource

Tax Services

Proactive Tax-Savings Plan

After a simple 20-30 minute, no-obligation assessment, we'll determine approximately how much we can reduce your tax burden. We will then do a deeper dive to decide if it makes sense for us to work together. We'll develop a tax savings plan utilizing our expert knowledge base. Your Proactive Tax Plan will provide a clear tax-reduction roadmap explicitly customized for you, your family, and your business that will stand up to IRS scrutiny.

Purpose-Driven Bookkeeping & Accounting

This goes well beyond the benefits of advisory and tax-preparation solutions. Hilton also helps you implement all recommended tax strategies with our complete bookkeeping and accounting services. Our exclusive methodology ensures that you achieve your tax plan's tax savings and that every expense is appropriately accounted for. We work closely with you to keep your books current and accurate.

Tax Fulfillment System

With the Tax Fulfillment System, you can choose the level that works best for you. Designed to fit any budget and circumstance, our exclusive suite of solutions *enables easy implementation* of the Tax Plan to help you put the tax savings right back into your pocket.

Advanced Tax Fulfillment System

Our Advanced Tax Fulfillment System includes all of the benefits and services of our Tax Fulfillment System but is designed to help higher-earning business owners as well as W2 employees that consistently earn over $500,000+ per year. This offering creates a unique, holistic strategy to ensure maximum tax savings and benefits for the client's family and dependents.

You can learn more about our full range of services at https://www.hiltonwealth.com/

About The Author

Mark Miller is the Manager of the Hilton Family Office and CEO of Hilton Tax & Wealth Advisors. He has been in the business financial consulting industry for over a quarter-century, working with hundreds of business owners, physicians, executives, and high net-worth individuals to increase their bottom line and financial security. Hilton and Miller offer practical and straightforward advice to cut long-term taxes, create iron-clad retirement plans, structure guaranteed income streams, grow business profits, and enhance personal wealth. They also offer uniquely designed financial strategies, providing high yields with quality surety.

Miller has attained Ethics Approved Status as a Registered Business Financial Consultant with the IARFC. He is also a best-selling author, having written several books on personal finance and best-in-class business-building practices. Over the years, he has been featured in over 200 newspapers and magazines such as The Kansas City Star, Kiplinger's

Personal Finance, Money Magazine, Women's Day, The New York Times, and the Los Angeles Daily News. Mark has also appeared as a business and financial expert on numerous radio and television shows nationwide, including Fox News.

Mark has been invited to Washington, DC, as a guest of several US Senators and Congresspersons. In 2006, he was among only 50 Americans to receive the coveted Businessman of the Year award from the Presidential Business Commission. That same year, he also received a personal commendation from President George W. Bush for his efforts to help Americans build their businesses and wealth.

Mark enjoys anything involving cars, planes, NFL football, golf, and NCAA basketball in his spare time. He is a member of the board of directors of his local church and heads up different initiatives in men's ministry.

Made in the USA
Columbia, SC
25 March 2024